My State
ILLINOIS

By Christina Earley

TABLE OF CONTENTS

A Crabtree Seedlings Book

Crabtree Publishing
crabtreebooks.com

School-to-Home Support for Caregivers and Teachers

This book helps children grow by letting them practice reading. Here are a few guiding questions to help the reader build his or her comprehension skills. Possible answers appear in red.

Before Reading:

- What do I know about Illinois?
    - *I know that Illinois is a state.*
    - *I know that Illinois is near the Mississippi River.*
- What do I want to learn about Illinois?
    - *I want to learn which famous people were born in Illinois.*
    - *I want to learn what the state flag looks like.*

During Reading:

- What have I learned so far?
    - *I have learned that Springfield is the state capital of Illinois.*
    - *I have learned that Chicago is the largest city in Illinois.*
- I wonder why...
    - *I wonder why the state flower is the common blue violet.*
    - *I wonder why the state park is called Starved Rock.*

After Reading:

- What did I learn about Illinois?
    - *I have learned that Six Flags Great America has big roller coasters.*
    - *I have learned that the state animal is the white-tailed deer.*
- Read the book again and look for the glossary words.
    - *I see the word **capital** on page 6, and the word **founder** on page 18. The other glossary words are found on pages 22 and 23.*

ILLINOIS
Hi! My name is Ayesha. Welcome to Illinois!

I live in Chicago. A river runs through my city.

Brownies and cell phones were **invented** here.

Illinois is in the **midwestern** United States. The **capital** is Springfield.

Fun Fact: Chicago is the largest city in Illinois.

The state animal is the white-tailed deer.

The common blue violet is the state flower.

We grow a lot of corn. Some of it is used to make corn muffins—my favorite!

Fun Fact: Illinois is one of the states that grows the most corn in the U.S.

My state flag is white. The state **seal** is in the middle.

There are six national sports teams in Illinois.

I like to visit Illinois Beach State Park in Zion. Sometimes we go fishing.

Fun Fact: More than 50 types of animals live on the beach.

I go **horseback** riding next to the Mississippi River in Pere Marquette State Park.

I have fun riding big roller coasters at Six Flags Great America.

Restaurant **pioneer** Ray Kroc, who owned McDonald's, was born in Illinois. Walt Disney was also born in Illinois.

Fun Fact: First Lady Michelle Obama was born in Chicago, Illinois.

In Springfield, I can visit the house where President Abraham Lincoln lived.

There are many waterfalls in Starved Rock State Park.

Glossary

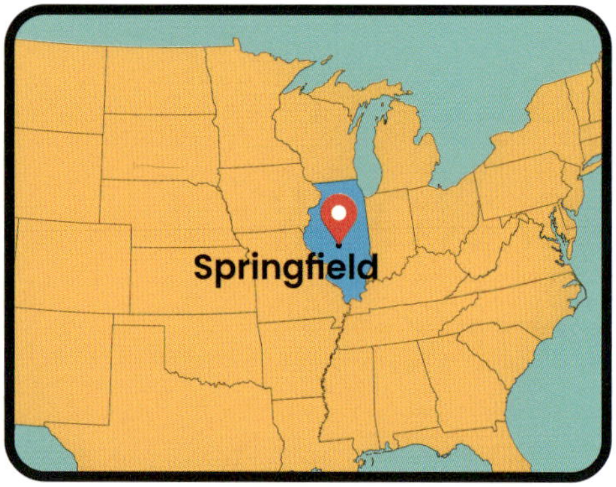

capital (cap-ih-tuhl): The city or town where the government of a country, state, or province is located

horseback (hors-back): On the back of a horse

invented (in-ven-tid): Created

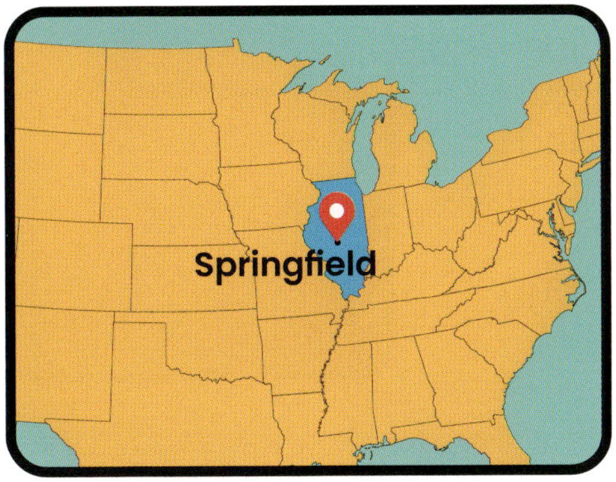

midwestern (mid-west-urn): The northern central part of the United States

pioneer (pahy-uh-neer): A person who is one of the first to do something

seal (seel): A special design that is used on important papers and other items

Index

About the Author

Christina Earley lives in sunny South Florida with her husband and son. She enjoys traveling around the United States and learning about different historical places. Her hobbies include hiking, yoga, and baking.

Written by: Christina Earley
Designed and Illustrated by: Bobbie Houser
Series Development: James Earley
Proofreader: Melissa Boyce
Educational Consultant: Marie Lemke M.Ed.

Photographs:
Alamy: Chuck Eckert: p. 17; Everett Collection Historical: p. 18 left, 23; HO Images: p. 18 right; White House Photo: p. 19
Newscom: David Seelig/Cal Sport Media: p. 13
Shutterstock: Photo Spirit: cover; Kenneth Keifer: p. 3; Rudy Balasko: p. 4; graham parton: p. 5 left, 22; Vasin Lee: p. 5 right, 22; Volina: p. 6, 22-23; Semmick Photo: p. 7; Tom Reichner: p. 8; Predrag Lukic: p. 9; Serg64: p. 10-11; Africa Studio: p. 11; Joseph Sohm: p. 12, 23; Jacob Boomsma: p. 14-15; Justin Russ: p. 15; TammiMild: p. 16, 22; Brett Welcher: p. 20; Tonya Kay: p. 21

Crabtree Publishing

crabtreebooks.com 800-387-7650

Printed in the U.S.A./012023/CG20220815

Published in Canada
Crabtree Publishing
616 Welland Avenue
St. Catharines, Ontario
L2M 5V6

Published in the United States
Crabtree Publishing
347 Fifth Avenue
Suite 1402-145
New York, New York, 10016

Library and Archives Canada Cataloguing in Publication
Available at Library and Archives Canada

Library of Congress Cataloging-in-Publication Data
Available at the Library of Congress

Hardcover: 978-1-0396-9657-0
Paperback: 978-1-0396-9764-5
Ebook (pdf): 978-1-0396-9978-6
Epub: 978-1-0396-9871-0